Copyright © 2025 by Meds Unplugged All rights reserved.

No part of this publication may be reproduced, stored or transmitted in any form or by any means, electronic, mechanical, photocopying, recording, scanning, or otherwise without written permission from the publisher. It is illegal to copy this book, post it to a website, or distribute it by any other means without permission.

Meds Unplugged asserts the moral right to be identified as the author of this work.

Designations used by companies to distinguish their products are often claimed as trademarks. All brand names and product names used in this book and on its cover are trade names, service marks, trademarks and registered trademarks of their respective owners. The publishers and the book are not associated with any product or vendor mentioned in this book. None of the companies referenced within the book have endorsed the book.

From Seed To Table

Contents

Introduction	5
Chapter 1: Planning Your Garden	7
Chapter 2: Selecting Your Seeds	9
Chapter 3: Planting and Growing	11
Chapter 4: Caring for Your Plants	13
Chapter 5: Harvesting and Storing Your Produce	15
Conclusion	17
My Gardening Journal	19

INTRODUCTION

A Beginner's Handbook to Harvesting Fresh Produce in Your Own Home

Welcome to your journey from Seed To Table! This handbook is crafted to guide you through the rewarding process of growing your own fresh produce at home. Whether you are an aspiring gardener or someone who simply loves fresh veggies, this book is designed to help you cultivate your gardening skills and enjoy the fruits of your labor.

In recent years, there' has been a growing interest in sustainable living and home gardening. Not only does growing your own food help reduce your carbon footprint, but it also ensures that you have access to fresh, organic produce right at your fingertips. This guide will take you through the basics of setting up your own home garden, selecting the right seeds, and caring for your plants until harvest. Whether you have a sprawling yard or a cozy balcony, starting a home garden can be both a fulfilling and environmentally friendly endeavor. By growing your own fruits, vegetables, and herbs, you gain a deeper connection to the food you eat and contribute to a healthier planet.

Let's delve into the essentials of home gardening, beginning with setting up your garden space. Evaluate your available area and consider factors such as sunlight, water access, and soil quality.

With thoughtful planning, even the smallest spaces can yield a significant bounty. Choosing the right seeds is the next crucial step. Opt for varieties that are well-suited to your climate and personal tastes. Whether you go for heirloom seeds with their rich history and flavor, or hybrids known for their resilience, each choice offers its own advantages. Once your seeds are selected, nurturing them into thriving plants is where the magic happens. From germination to growth, each stage requires attention and care. Regular watering, appropriate fertilization, and protection against pests are all part of ensuring a healthy garden.

Finally, when the time for harvest arrives, the rewards of your labor are tangible and delicious. There's nothing quite like the taste of freshly picked produce, and sharing it with family and friends adds to the joy. Embark on this journey with enthusiasm and curiosity, and you'll soon find that gardening is not just a hobby but a way of life that enriches both your table and your soul.

ALL THE TOOLS YOU'LL NEED

- MAKE IT A FAMILY EXPERIENCE
- CREATE A JOURNAL
- LOVE & PATIENCE → WATERING CAN
- GLOVES
- GARDEN BOOTS
- SHOVEL
- SEEDS
- RAKE
- TROWEL
- SOIL ↑ REPEAT!

WWW.REALLYGREATSITE.COM @REALLYGREATSITE

CHAPTER ONE

Chapter 1: Planning Your Garden

1.1 Choosing the Right Location
Selecting the perfect spot for your garden is crucial. Consider the amount of sunlight, availability of water, and soil quality. A sunny location with at least 6-8 hours of direct sunlight is ideal for most vegetables. Observe the area throughout the day to identify the sunniest spots, and avoid places that are overly shaded by trees or buildings.

1.2 Understanding Your Climate Zone
Different plants thrive in different climates. Learn about your local climate zone, which is determined by factors such as temperature, rainfall, and seasonal changes. Resources like the USDA Plant Hardiness Zone Map can help you identify your zone and choose plants that are well-suited to your region's weather conditions.

1.3 Designing Your Garden Layout
Decide between raised beds, container gardening, or traditional rows. Each method has its own benefits and challenges:

- **Raised Beds**: Great for improving soil drainage and reducing weeds. They allow for better soil control and can be easier on your back.

- **Container Gardening**: Ideal for small spaces or patios, containers can be moved to optimize sunlight and protect plants from harsh weather.

- **Traditional Rows**: A classic approach, this method works well for larger plots but can require more maintenance.

Choose the one that fits best with your available space and resources, considering factors lsuch as accessibility and aesthetics.

PLANT THE SEEDS AND WAIT FOR THE HARVEST

ITS HARVEST TIME

1.4 Gathering the Necessary Tools

Having the right tools on hand will make your gardening experience more enjoyable and efficient. Basic tools you'll need include a spade, trowel, garden fork, hoe, watering can, and gloves. For larger gardens, consider investing in a wheelbarrow for easy transportation of soil and compost. Quality tools can last for years, so select durable, comfortable options.

Planning

1.5 Planning for Crop Rotation

Crop rotation is a practice that helps to maintain healthy soil and reduce pest and disease buildup. Plan your garden layout with rotation in mind, and avoid planting the same family of plants in the same spot year after year. This encourages nutrient balance and disrupts pest life cycles. Keep a garden journal to track plant locations and make adjustments for future seasons.

1.6 Setting Realistic Goals

As you embark on your gardening journey, set realistic expectations. Start small, focusing on a few select crops that you and your family will enjoy. This will help you learn the basics without becoming overwhelmed. As your skills and confidence grow, you can gradually expand your garden to include a broader variety of crops. Remember, gardening is a learning process, and each season offers new opportunities for discovery and growth.

The Importance Of Planning

Planning before you start is like a blue print for your gardeing project. It sets the foundation for success and ensures that your efforts yield the best possible results. Begin by assessing your available space, considering factors such as sunlight exposure, soil quality, and water access. Sketch out a rough plan of your garden,, taking into account the needs of each plant type, including their spacing and growth habits.

Think about seasonal changes and how they will affect your garden. For instance, some plants thrive in cooler weather, while others require the warmth of summer to flourish. By aligning your planting schedule with the natural cycles of your climate, you can maximize your harvest and enjoy a continuous supply of fresh produce.

Additionally, take into account your time and resources. Determine how much time you can realistically dedicate to your garden each week and plan accordingly. Having a well-thought-out plan will not only save you time and effort but also make your gardening journey more enjoyable and rewarding.

CHAPTER 2: SELECTING YOUR SEEDS

2.1 Heirloom vs. Hybrid Seeds
Understanding the differences between heirloom and hybrid seeds is essential for making informed choices:

- *Heirloom Seeds: Open-pollinated and often passed down through generations, these seeds tend to have rich flavors and unique characteristics.*

- *Hybrid Seeds: Bred for specific traits such as disease resistance or increased yield, hybrids can produce a more uniform crop but may lack the diversity and flavor of heirloom varieties.*

2.2 Deciding What to Grow
Consider your family's preferences, the season, and the space available. Start with easy-to-grow vegetables like tomatoes, lettuce, or carrots if you're new to gardening. Also, think about companion planting, which involves growing different plants together for mutual benefits, such as pest control or improved growth.

2.3 Sourcing Quality Seeds
When it comes to sourcing seeds, quality is key. Look for reputable seed companies that offer organic and non-GMO options. Local nurseries and garden centers can also be valuable resources, providing seeds that are well-suited to your region's climate. Additionally, seed exchanges and community gardening groups can offer heirloom varieties that are adapted to local conditions, often accompanied by helpful growing tips from seasoned gardeners.

2.4 Reading Seed Packets

Seed packets contain a wealth of information to guide your planting process. Pay attention to details such as planting depth, spacing, germination time, and sun requirements. Understanding these instructions will help ensure successful germination and healthy growth. Seed packets may also include helpful tips for optimal care and harvesting, making them a handy reference throughout the growing season.

2.5 Starting Seeds Indoors vs. Direct Sowing

Decide whether to start seeds indoors or sow them directly into the garden. Starting seeds indoors allows you to get a head start on the growing season, particularly for plants that require a longer growing period or warmer temperatures. On the other hand, direct sowing is convenient for quick-growing plants or those that don't transplant well. Consider your climate, the specific needs of each plant, and your available space when making this decision.

2.6 Keeping a Seed Journal

Maintaining a seed journal can be an invaluable tool for tracking your gardening progress. Record details like seed varieties, planting dates, germination success, and any challenges you encounter. This practice not only helps you learn from each season but also allows you to refine your approach over time. As you build your gardening knowledge, your journal will become a personalized guide to achieving fruitful harvests year after year.

CHAPTER 3
PLANTING & GROWING

PREPARING THE SOIL

3.1 Preparing the Soil
Healthy soil is the foundation of a successful garden. Start with soil testing to determine its pH and nutrient levels. Amend your soil as needed with compost, manure, or fertilizers to enhance its fertility. Properly prepare your soil by tilling or turning it to ensure aeration and drainage.

SOWING SEEDS

3.2 Sowing Seeds and Transplanting
Get step-by-step instructions on how to sow seeds directly into the soil or start them indoors for transplanting later. Follow the seed packet instructions for planting depth and spacing, and ensure you harden off any seedlings started indoors before planting them outside.

WATERING & FERTILIZING

3.3 Watering and Fertilization
Discover the importance of watering schedules and nutrient-rich fertilizers to ensure your plants grow strong and healthy. Water early in the morning or late in the afternoon to minimize evaporation. Consider using drip irrigation or soaker hoses to deliver moisture directly to the root zone. Consistent watering is crucial, as both overwatering and underwatering can stress plants and hinder their growth. Monitor your garden regularly to adjust watering practices based on weather conditions and plant needs. Fertilization should be tailored to the specific requirements of your plants; organic options like compost tea or fish emulsion can provide a gentle, balanced nutrient boost.

A GARDEN A DAY KEEPS THE DOCTOR AWAY!

3.4 Supporting and Training Plants

Many plants, especially vining varieties like tomatoes or cucumbers, benefit from support structures such as stakes, cages, or trellises. These supports help keep plants upright, improve air circulation, and make harvesting easier. Train your plants early by gently guiding them to grow along their support systems. Regularly check and adjust ties to prevent damage to stems as plants grow.

3.5 Weeding and Mulching

Weeds compete with your plants for water, nutrients, and sunlight, so it's important to keep them under control. Regularly inspect your garden for weeds and remove them by hand or with a hoe. Applying a layer of mulch around your plants can help suppress weed growth, retain soil moisture, and regulate soil temperature. Organic mulches like straw, wood chips, or shredded leaves also contribute to soil health as they decompose.

3.6 Monitoring Plant Growth

Keep a close eye on your plants' development to catch any issues early. Look for signs of nutrient deficiencies, pest infestations, or diseases. Take note of any abnormal growth patterns or discoloration. By being proactive, you can address problems before they escalate, ensuring your garden remains healthy and productive. Regularly document your observations in your gardening journal to track progress and make informed adjustments.

CHAPTER 4
CARING FOR YOUR PLANTS

4.1 Pest and Disease Management
Identify common garden pests and diseases and learn eco-friendly methods to keep them at bay. Introduce beneficial insects like ladybugs and lacewings, and consider using organic pesticides or natural repellents to protect your plants without harming the environment.

4.2 Pruning and Maintenance
Regular pruning and maintenance are key to healthy plant growth. Find out how to properly care for your plants to maximize yield. Remove dead or yellowing leaves, and pinch back growing tips to encourage bushier plants. Mulching can also help retain moisture and suppress weeds. Consistent attention to your garden will ensure that your plants remain in optimal health, leading to a more productive harvest. Regularly inspect your plants for any signs of stress or irregular growth, as early intervention is often the most effective.

4.3 Soil Health and Composting
Maintaining soil health is fundamental to successful gardening. Composting is a great way to enrich your soil with organic matter, enhancing its structure, nutrient content, and water retention capabilities. Collect kitchen scraps, garden clippings, and fallen leaves to create a rich compost that will act as a natural fertilizer. Regularly turn your compost pile to speed up decomposition and ensure even breakdown of materials.

4.4 Seasonal Adjustments
Adapt your gardening practices to fit the changing seasons. As temperatures shift, adjust your watering schedule and consider using row covers or cold frames to protect plants from frost. Rotate crops at the end of each season to prevent soil depletion and break pest cycles. Seasonal adjustments keep your garden productive and your plants resilient throughout the year.

4.5 Encouraging Pollinators

Pollinators like bees, butterflies, and hummingbirds play a crucial role in the health of your garden. Encourage these helpful creatures by planting a variety of flowering plants that bloom at different times. Avoid using harsh chemicals that could harm these valuable allies, and consider providing habitats like bee hotels or small water sources to support their presence.

By dedicating time to care for your plants thoughtfully and sustainably, you're not only ensuring a successful garden but also contributing to a healthier ecosystem. With patience and dedication, you'll create a thriving environment capable of providing fresh produce and a sense of fulfillment.

FROM SEED TO TABLE   A BDGINNER'S GUIDE FOR
                                       GROWING NATURAL
                                              FOOOS

HARVEST TIME

Chapter 5: Harvesting and Storing Your Produce

5.1 Knowing When to Harvest
Learn to recognize the signs that your produce is ready for harvest to ensure the best flavor and texture. Each crop has specific indicators, such as size, color, and firmness. Research your plants to know the optimal harvesting times.

5.2 Techniques for Harvesting
Proper harvesting techniques are important to avoid damaging your plants. Use sharp, clean tools like scissors or pruners for cutting, and handle your produce gently to prevent bruising. Harvest in the morning for the freshest flavors.

5.3 Storing Fresh Produce
Once harvested, learn how to store your produce to prolong freshness and enjoy your bounty for longer. Different vegetables require different storage methods—some do well in the refrigerator, while others might prefer a cool, dark place. Be mindful of how to handle each type of produce to maintain quality. Proper storage begins with understanding the unique needs of each type of produce. For instance, leafy greens like lettuce and spinach benefit from being wrapped in a damp cloth and stored in the "crisper" drawer of the refrigerator, while root vegetables such as carrots and beets can be kept in a perforated plastic bag. Tomatoes, on the other hand, are best stored at room temperature until they fully ripen.

5.4 Preserving Your Harvest

If you have an abundant harvest, consider preserving some of your produce through methods like canning, freezing, or drying. Canning is ideal for tomatoes, cucumbers, and peppers, transforming them into sauces, pickles, or relishes. Freezing is a great option for berries, peas, and corn, preserving their nutrients and flavors. Drying herbs like basil, oregano, and thyme provides a long-lasting way to enjoy their aromatic qualities throughout the year.

5.5 Sharing Your Bounty

Sharing the fruits of your labor can be one of the most gratifying aspects of gardening. Consider swapping produce with neighbors, donating excess to local food banks, or hosting a community potluck to celebrate the harvest. Engaging with your community this way not only reduces waste but also fosters a sense of connection and shared appreciation for fresh, homegrown food.

5.6 Reflecting on the Season

As the growing season winds down, take time to reflect on your gardening experiences. Note what worked well and what could be improved, and update your gardening journal with these observations. This reflection will help you plan for future seasons and continue your growth as a gardener. Celebrate your achievements, no matter how small, and look forward to the next cycle of planting and harvesting.

| FROM SEED TO TABLE | A BEGINNER'S GUIDE TO GROWING NATRUAL FOODS |

Conclusion

Enjoy The Journey

Gardening is a rewarding endeavor that reconnects us with nature and the food we consume. With patience and practice, anyone can transform their home into a thriving garden. Remember, every gardener was once a beginner, and with this handbook, you're well on your way to becoming an expert in growing your own food from *Seed To Table*.

Enjoy your gardening journey! Whether you're tending to a small balcony garden or a spacious backyard plot, the skills and knowledge that you have acquired will serve as the foundation for a lifetime of sustainable, delicious, and fulfilling harvests. Embrace the challenges and triumphs that come with each planting season, and always remember to savor the simple joys of nurturing life from the soil.

As you continue to explore the world of gardening, consider sharing your experiences and newfound wisdom with others. Inspire friends and family to embark on their own gardening adventures, fostering a community of passionate growers who support and learn from one another. Together, we can cultivate not only gardens but also a more sustainable and connected world.

Happy Gardening! May your future harvests be bountiful and your journey be as enriching as the soil you tend!

My Gardening Journal

My Gardening Journal

My Gardening Journal

My Gardening Journal

My Gardening Journal

My Gardening Journal

My Gardening Journal

My Gardening Journal

My Gardening Journal

My Gardening Journal

My Gardening Journal

My Gardening Journal

My Gardening Journal

My Gardening Journal

My Gardening Journal

My Gardening Journal

www.ingramcontent.com/pod-product-compliance
Lightning Source LLC
LaVergne TN
LVHW060133080526
838201LV00118B/3041